SHIRE NATURAL

THE
COMMON SEAL

PAUL THOMPSON

CONTENTS

Cover: *A common seal haul-out group in Orkney.*

Series editor: Jim Flegg.

Set in 9 point Times roman and printed in Great Britain by C. I. Thomas & Sons (Haverfordwest) Ltd, Press Buildings, Merlins Bridge, Haverfordwest, Dyfed.

Introduction

The common seal (*Phoca vitulina*) is one of 34 species of seal which occur throughout the world. Along with the grey seal (*Halichoerus grypus*), it is a member of the family Phocidae or true seals. These phocid seals are characterised by their fur-covered flippers, the absence of external ear pinnae, and hind flippers which cannot be turned forwards. This last characteristic allows them to swim powerfully by thrusting their hind flippers back and forth but makes them rather cumbersome when they haul out (the term given to their behaviour when they come out of the water on to land). In contrast, fur seals and sea-lions of the family Otariidae can turn their hind flippers forwards, allowing them to stand relatively upright on four 'legs', a feature which has resulted in their use as circus performers. Other characteristics of the otariids are their external ear pinnae and their larger fore flippers, which they use as their primary means of propulsion. Unlike phocids, male otariids have testes which are in a scrotal sac, external to the body wall. The third family of seals, the Odobenidae, contains only one species, the walrus. Walruses share certain characteristics with seals from both the other families but are best distinguished by their almost naked skin and enlarged upper canines which form a pair of huge tusks.

Common seals are one of the smaller species of phocids, growing to a maximum length of around 1.75 metres and weighing up to about 130 kilograms. The sexes differ in size, or are dimorphic, with mature males weighing about 25 per cent more than females. Males are also more heavily built, particularly around the neck, where they may often be scarred. Despite this difference in size, the sexes are most reliably identified by observation of their genitalia, as younger males are often of a similar size and build to females. The genitalia can normally be seen at reasonably close range, if seals are lying out of the water with their bellies towards the observer. In both sexes there is an obvious umbilical scar on the midline of the body. Between this scar and the anus, either the male's penile opening, surrounded by stiff hairs, or, less obviously, the female's pair of nipples can be seen.

Apart from the occasional arctic vagrant, the only other species of seal to be found in British waters is the grey seal. Nevertheless, identifying the two species can often be difficult as, in many areas, they share the same habitat and may form mixed haul-out groups. Adults can be distinguished most readily by their head shape, the common seal having a snub nose and rather rounded head compared with the grey seal's straight 'Roman' nose. Some young grey seals can, however, have quite a short face, which may lead to confusion. Size can also be useful, with full-grown grey seals weighing almost twice as much as common seals of the same sex, but there is considerable overlap between common seals and younger grey seals. When looked at head-on at short range, the shape of the nostrils is helpful diagnostically: common seals have V-shaped nostrils which almost touch at the bottom, whereas the grey seal's are more parallel.

At a distance it is more difficult to separate the two species. The pelage pattern is sometimes useful but may lead to confusion when either species is about to moult: both grey and common seal coats may turn a muddy brown colour at this time. Outside the moult period, common seals tend to have a much finer spot pattern in contrast to the grey seal's larger black splodges. The spacing of individuals within a group can also be a useful feature when trying to identify seals on their haul-out sites. Common seals tend to space themselves out widely on land and if two seals get too close together they will threaten each other. On the other hand, grey seals tolerate each other much more when hauled out together and often form tightly bunched groups. These closely spaced groups of grey seals are always single-species groups, but the odd grey seal may often be seen within the more spaced-out groups of common seals.

All in all, unless one is close enough to see the nostrils clearly, no one characteristic is reliable enough to be used alone to

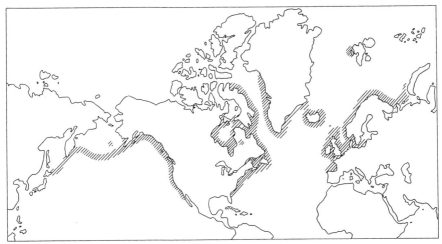

1. *The world distribution of the common seal (Phoca vitulina).*

distinguish between the two species. Instead, several of the features described may be needed in order to deduce the identity of a particular individual.

Distribution

Common seals are one of the most widely distributed of pinnipeds, occurring along the temperate, sub-arctic and arctic coasts of the North Pacific and North Atlantic. They are most easily seen when they haul out and, consequently, most information on their distribution relates to haul-out groups, with relatively little being known about where seals go when they are feeding at sea.

Five subspecies are generally recognised, but all are very similar and their validity is rather uncertain. Differences between them are based largely on their geographical distribution, and only slight morphological variations exist in their size, skull characteristics and pelage pattern. In the eastern North Atlantic *Phoca vitulina vitulina* is occasionally found as far south as the coast of Portugal and occurs regularly further north around the European coast up to Iceland and Spitzbergen. *P.v. concolor* occurs along the western shore of the North Atlantic, from

northern Florida to Hudson Bay and Baffin Island, and across to west and south-eastern Greenland. One subspecies, *P.v. mellonae*, occurs in fresh water and lives 150 km (90 miles) inland in the landlocked Seal Lakes east of Hudson Bay. Finally, two subspecies occur in the North Pacific: *P.v. richardsi* on the east, from Baja California up to western Alaska, and *P.v. stejnegeri* in the west, around northern Japan and the Kamchatka peninsula. The spotted seal (*P. largha*) is a close relative of the common seal and was once thought to be a further subspecies. It breeds on the ice in the North Pacific and its range partially overlaps with that of the common seal in this area.

HABITAT
Throughout their range, common seals are found in a wide variety of coastal habitats, coming ashore on sandbanks, rocky shores, ice-floes and even oil pipelines or other man-made objects. Around the coast of Britain they are most abundant in Scotland, particularly on the west coast and around the Hebrides, Orkney and Shetland. Here they are often seen hauled out on rocky beaches or offshore skerries, often surpisingly close to roads, harbours and human habitation. Their distribution is more restricted on the east coast of Britain, but they do occur in

3

several of the east coast estuaries from the Moray Firth in the north of Scotland down to the Wash and the Thames in the south of England. In these estuarine areas seals normally come ashore and rest on sandbanks which are exposed at low tide, tending to use banks where there is easy access to deep water. In large estuaries such as the Wash, this can make observing them from the shore difficult. Often, however, local boat trips may take visitors out near the sandbanks to see seals at close range while, on the smaller estuaries on the east coast of Scotland, seals can be seen from roads running along the coast. Occasionally they are also seen along the English south and west coasts and they have a much greater tendency than grey seals to wander inland up rivers. Most notably, common seals have been sighted in the river Thames above Tower Bridge and in several Scottish lochs, including Loch Ness.

SITE USE

Unlike several other species of seal, common seals do not undertake a major annual migration but appear to remain around preferred areas of coast throughout the year. Nevertheless, within some of these areas there do seem to be seasonal changes in the use of particular haul-out sites. Certain sites are used mainly during the breeding season; at some of these females and their pups predominate, while groups of seals seen at other breeding-season sites contain mostly males. During the winter, these breeding sites are often deserted and seals move to alternative haul-out sites, although it is not known to what extent the sexes segregate at this time of year. The reasons for such changes in site use are not fully understood. In some parts of North America, seasonal movements between haul-out sites appear to be related to changes in feeding areas. On the other hand, studies in Orkney have shown that winter and breeding-season haul-out sites are sometimes within a few kilometres of each other. Seals in these areas are known to travel further than this to feed, sometimes swimming past an alternative haul-out site as they return from a feeding trip. Therefore, it seems unlikely that seasonal changes in site use are a result of

2. *Common seals leave distinctive tracks when disturbed from their sandbank haul-out sites.*

3. *An adult female grey seal on the Isle of May, off the coast of Fife.*

seasonal movements between different feeding grounds. Instead, females may be choosing remoter sites at which to give birth and feed their pups or, alternatively, seals may be using more sheltered sites during the winter.

Movements between different haul-out sites have been studied in a number of areas by marking seals so that individuals can be recognised. In some cases numbered plastic or metal tags have been placed in the webbing of the hind flippers, while other studies have used paint or dye to put larger marks or numbers on the seal's pelage. More recently, radio transmitters have been developed which can withstand salt-water immersion and the pressure resulting from deep dives. These radio tags have been glued to the hair on the seal's back or attached to ankle bracelets and used to study both the seals' movements and their behaviour. Because the radio waves can be heard only when seals are at the surface, it is possible to distinguish whether the individual is in the water or hauled out on land. These studies have shown that adult common seals can remain very faithful to particular haul-out sites, moving around the same group of favoured sites on a seasonal basis over a number of years. In contrast, individuals which have been tagged as pups or juveniles often move much greater distances, some which were tagged at sites in Britain having dispersed right across the North Sea (figure 5). As with many other mammals, these longer movements by pups are probably exploratory and dispersal movements to other breeding populations. Once seals have become established in an area, it appears that they continue to use that area for many years.

Although tagging studies have greatly increased our knowledge of the way in which individual common seals use different haul-out sites, we still know very little about their social relationships. Common seal haul-out groups were once thought to be societies of strangers, mainly because few overt interactions were seen between individuals within a group. The fact that known individuals are very faithful to particular sites, and sometimes even to specific areas within a site, does, however, suggest that their social organisation is probably more complex than was previously believed.

Population size and dynamics

SURVEY METHODS

Almost all estimates of common seal population size are based on counts which have been made at their terrestrial haul-out sites. In some cases these counts have been carried out by observers on land, in others from boats and, over larger areas, aerial censuses have been made. The accuracy with which the number of seals ashore can be estimated by these methods varies considerably. In addition, they share one common problem: because an unknown number of seals will have remained in the water during the survey, the count of visible animals represents only a minimum estimate of the population size. If the proportion of the population which was ashore during each survey period remained constant, this would not necessarily cause too many problems. The total population size would remain unknown, but haul-out counts would at least provide a useful index of population size. This index could then be used to give an indication of whether a population was stable or was changing in size over a period of years. Unfortunately though, studies have shown that the frequency with which common seals haul out can vary enormously, depending on a wide variety of factors such as weather conditions, levels of disturbance and even the ages or sex of the individual seals concerned. In particular, haul-out behaviour appears to vary according to the time of year, so timing becomes critical if the results of several surveys are to be compared. Common seals appear to spend the highest proportion of their time hauled out of the water during the moult (see the next chapter). Surveys carried out at this time of year are therefore likely to produce the highest minimum population estimates, and those closest to the real population size. Furthermore, the seals' behaviour appears to be more predictable during the moult, and radio-tracking techniques can be used to estimate how long individual seals spend ashore during the periods when surveys

4. *A juvenile common seal which has been tagged on one of its flippers in order that its movements between haul-out sites may be studied.*

5. *A map showing the dispersal movement of common seal pups which have been tagged in the Wash and in Orkney.*

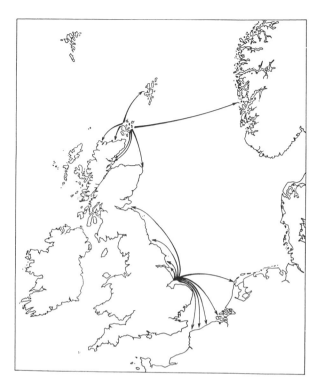

are carried out. These data can then be used to produce correction factors for counts to allow for the proportion of the seal population which is likely to be in the water during surveys. However, because scientists in different countries, and even in different parts of the same country, have used a number of different survey techniques over previous years, it is still not yet possible to produce a meaningful estimate for the size of the world's common seal population.

POPULATION SIZE

In Britain a number of survey techniques have been used to count common seals since about 1970. For the reasons outlined above it is not possible to say whether the population is stable or whether, like the British grey seal population, it is increasing. Nevertheless, surveys do provide minimum estimates for the population in different areas. Most British common seals are found around the Scottish coast, with minimum population estimates in 1985 of 4500 for the west coast and Inner Hebrides, 1300 for the Outer Hebrides, 4700 for Shetland, 6600 for Orkney and 1000 for the east coast estuaries. In Ireland there are believed to be at least 1500 common seals, with most of these occurring in the north and the remaining animals scattered down the west coast. On the English coast, although small numbers occur in other east coast estuaries, the only significant population is in the Wash. Mark and recapture studies were carried out on the Wash population in the early 1970s, when over five hundred pups were tagged over a period of several years. At that time commercial hunters were taking pups from this population for their skins. The proportion of tagged pups which were present amongst the sample of pups killed by these hunters was therefore used to produce an estimate of the pup production for the area. The resulting total population estimate for the Wash of around 6600 was found to be much larger than the highest haul-out counts of 1722 individuals. Similarly, more recent radio-tracking studies in Orkney suggest that the total population size there is considerably greater than previous minimum estimates from counts at haul-out sites. Thus it is likely that the British common seal population is much larger than the minimum estimates suggest.

POPULATION DYNAMICS

Juvenile common seals can generally be recognised from their small size and the colour of their coat, which becomes pale fawn when dry. Once they are over one year old, however, it is impossible to age them reliably from external characteristics. Methods for estimating the age of older seals are available only for dead individuals, which can be aged by taking out a tooth, sectioning it and counting the annual growth rings in the cementum. Consequently, most data which are available on the age structure of common seal populations, and on other population parameters, relate to North America, where bounty schemes have resulted in a large number of carcasses for study.

Although population parameters are likely to vary slightly between exploited and unexploited populations of the same species, these North American studies provide the best available data for the British common seal population.

Mortality. Data on mortality rates for all age-classes are poor but are especially lacking for young seals. One study in Canada suggested that at least 12 per cent of pups died in their first year of life, while theoretical models for the Dutch population suggest that mortality may reach 50 to 60 per cent in the first year. Whatever the exact figures, as for other mammal populations it is likely that a high proportion of pups do not survive beyond their first few months of life. For those seals which do live beyond this, mortality rates are initially similar for both sexes and, for common seals from birth to five years old, the sex-ratio remains approximately 1:1. Amongst older seals males die at a greater rate, probably due to the additional risks resulting from competition amongst themselves for access to breeding females. This results in an increasingly

6. *A female common seal. Some females may live to be over thirty years old.*

8

7. *A group of common seals at a typical rocky shore haul-out site in Orkney.*

8. *Common seals hauled out on an inter-tidal sandbank.*

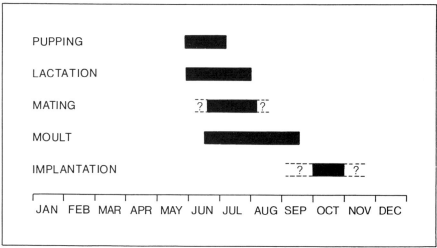

PUPPING

LACTATION

MATING   ?   ?

MOULT

IMPLANTATION   ?   ?

JAN FEB MAR APR MAY JUN JUL AUG SEP OCT NOV DEC

9. *The timing of the major events in the common seal's annual cycle.*

skewed sex-ratio, so that males are likely to live only up to twenty years old, while females may reach the age of thirty.

Throughout much of the common seal's range natural predators other than man are rare. Nevertheless, remains have been found in the stomachs of marine predators such as white sharks (*Carcharodon carcharias*) and killer whales (*Orcinus orca*). Killer whales have even been seen taking seals in British waters, but this is too rare an event to have any significant effect on a population level. Terrestrial predators and predatory birds such as great black-backed gulls (*Larus marinus*) may also kill young pups at haul-out sites, but these pups are likely to be weak individuals which are already sick or have been abandoned.

Little is known of other causes of mortality, such as disease. Juvenile common seals are seen regularly with raw lesions, often around their umbilicus, but it is not known whether this condition is normally fatal. They also harbour large numbers of parasites: ectoparasites such as lice, and various species of nematode, acanthocephalan and cestode worms in the gut are particularly common. In most cases these are unlikely to cause serious problems, but lung worms are also found frequently, and these are believed to be a significant cause of mortality in some populations. It also appears that common seals occasionally succumb to epidemic diseases. In Shetland in the 1920s large numbers of seals were found dead and dying from an unknown disease and in 1988 an epidemic believed to be caused by a virus like canine distemper killed several thousand common seals around North Sea coasts.

Reproduction. Reproductive rates for common seals are based on studies of the reproductive tracts of individuals which have been shot by hunters. Mature males can be identified during the breeding season either by the presence of sperm in the sperm-storage tube, the epididymis, or by the rapid increase in the size of testes and epididymis tubules which occurs at sexual maturity. Using these criteria, it appears that most male common seals reach sexual maturity between the ages of five and six years old. However, although they become physically mature at this age it may be much later before they become socially mature and mate successfully. Females, on the other hand, show signs of their first ovulation at a younger age: on average when they are only three or four years old. An estimated 80 per cent of the younger females are then likely to produce pups in any one year, compared with over 95 per cent of females of seven years or older.

The annual cycle

Common seals have clearly defined annual cycles in their breeding and moulting biology. Although there is little difference in the timing of these cycles among seals around the British coast, there are marked variations within and between other populations. Along the Pacific coast of North America, for example, pups in California are born as early as April, whereas females in British Columbia do not pup until September. The reasons for such differences are not fully understood, but they are probably due partly to variations in food availability. In particular, it may be important for there to be a rich supply of food, such as shrimps or small fish, which are easy prey for the young pups when they become independent from their mothers.

In the following account of the annual cycle most information applies to common seals worldwide, but details on timing are based on the British population.

PUPPING

By late May female common seals are heavily pregnant and have a thick layer of blubber as a result of their intensive feeding activity during the winter. In the subsequent weeks they will come ashore more regularly than at any other time of year. Time for feeding is therefore limited, and these fat reserves are essential if their pups are to be fed adequately.

Pupping is highly synchronous and most births occur in early to mid June. The timing of the common seal's pupping period is therefore quite different from that of the grey seal, which produces its pups between September and December. During the pupping period, and throughout lactation, common seal females tend to group together and use different haul-out sites to the majority of males. Immediately prior to giving birth they move away from other seals, often to the edge of these groups, to minimise disturbance while they are in labour or with their very young pup.

Although extremely vulnerable when on land in their first day or so, the pups are more advanced at birth than most other species of seal. Except in a few rare cases, the white pre-natal coat or lanugo, which grey seal pups retain for some time after birth, is moulted in the uterus and expelled with the placenta. Common seal pups are therefore born in their first adult coat and are able to swim and dive for up to several minutes in their first hour of life. It is this ability which has allowed the species to exploit estuarine habitats for breeding, as haul-out sites in these areas are often available at low tide only. It also makes pups less vulnerable to terrestrial predators, such as man, as mothers can retreat to the safety of the water with them when disturbed. Consequently, common seals are frequently found breeding in areas frequented by

10. *A female playing with her pup in the water.*

11

11. *Common seals coming ashore at an Orkney haul-out site.*

12. *A young common seal, showing the pale unpatterned pelage typical of juveniles, with an adult in the background.*

13. *A female common seal hauled out with her pup in Shetland.*

14. *A young common seal pup in Orkney.*

15. *A pup feeding from its mother.*

16. *Mothers keep in close contact with their pups, both in and out of the water.*

14

17. *Weed flinging is often an important part of the aquatic displays seen during the breeding season.*

humans, whereas other species may be restricted to uninhabited offshore islands.

During the three to four week lactation period pups more than double their birth weight of around 10 kilograms. Females produce an extremely fat-rich milk, which the pups lay down to form a thick blubber layer. Early in the lactation period mothers and pups remain in close contact. They come ashore to suckle and to rest but regularly return to the water, even when they are not forced to do so by high tides. In the water, mothers frequently nuzzle the pups to maintain contact and even give 'piggyback' rides to support them at the surface. It is at this age that common seals are most vocal, with pups frequently giving a high-pitched contact call to keep in touch with their mothers. Other than these pup calls, one hears common seals make only the occasional growl, normally as part of a threat gesture when another individual comes too close on the haul-out site.

How much time the mothers and pups spend feeding during this period is not known. Females lose considerable mass during lactation and look extremely thin by the time the pup is weaned. It therefore seems likely that feeding activity is restricted severely while they have to remain close inshore with their pups. Even if the female's food consumption is negligible, her time in the water with the pup may provide vital feeding experience. As weaning approaches, the pups are left ashore for longer periods while females spend time at sea, apparently feeding. Weaning marks the end of a brief but intensive relationship and the pup has to learn to feed proficiently on its own, with only its blubber reserves to rely upon if it is slow to learn.

MATING

Observations of mating behaviour are extremely rare as, unlike most other seals, common seals mate in the water. Consequently, in order to determine when mating occurs, indirect indications of mating have had to be used. Studies of female reproductive tracts, taken from animals sampled throughout the year, have shown that ovulation occurs in July, around the time of weaning. At this time of year there is also a peak in the incidence of wounds on mature male common seals, apparently due to intense male-male competition. There is, however, surprisingly little aggression between males when they are on the haul-out sites. Most competitive interactions therefore appear to occur in the water, where pairs of animals are sometimes seen grappling with each other, each individual with its jaws locked around the other's throat. Many of the wounds seen on males at this time are multiple short

15

18. *A female common seal rebuffs a male's attempt to mate with her on land.*

cuts around the neck and appear to be bite wounds inflicted during these fights. Large males often have very tattered webbing and lost or damaged claws on their hind flippers, possibly also resulting from fights between males. A variety of aquatic displays are associated with this aggressive male behaviour. These include rolling sidways at the surface and slapping the water with a fore flipper to produce a rifle-shot sound, and displacement activities such as shaking a piece of kelp in the air. It is also possible that more complex underwater displays take place, but only the parts of these which occur at the surface have been described. Similar behaviours are also seen as an element of juvenile play, but their interactions tend to be more congenial and often last for much longer periods.

Because of the lack of observations of mating pairs, it is difficult to obtain a clear picture of the common seal's mating system. Although they were once thought to be monogamous, it is now clear that males play no part in rearing pups and that they are probably serially polygynous. In other words, although a breeding male does not hold a harem of females at any one time, he probably mates with a number of females in succession. Exactly how males manage to obtain successful matings with several females remains unclear. During July, males are occasionally seen coming ashore and approaching females which

are hauled out on the beach. After a slow approach, the male may suddenly attempt to grab the female by the back of the neck and force a copulation. In all recorded accounts of this behaviour, however, the female fought off the male and he failed to mate with her. These observations, together with descriptions of mating behaviour in captive seals, suggest that mating normally occurs in the water and is likely to be successful only with the co-operation of the female. Females therefore appear to have a high degree of choice over where, when and with which male they mate, and it seems likely that the male displays and fights seen in the water may serve to attract females.

Although females ovulate and are mated during July, the fertilised egg does not implant in the uterine wall immediately. Instead, development of the blastocyst is suspended for around two or three months, during which it remains free in the upper part of the uterus. Eventually, development resumes and the blastocyst becomes attached to the uterine wall. This period of 'delayed implantation' is also found in other species of seal and in a few terrestrial mammals such as the badger (*Meles meles*).

MOULT

Soon after the breeding season, common seals undergo a complete annual

19. *A mature male, with recent neck wounds from fights with other males, approaching a female. A young grey seal watches in the background.*

20. *When two common seals get too close to each other on a haul-out site, it often leads to threatening behaviour and sometimes a short fight.*

moult which, for some individuals, can last until mid September. In the early stages of moult, the coat appears dull and brown. Hair loss normally occurs first around the face and body openings and then spreads along the belly to other regions. As the old hair is shed, generally in a fairly patchy manner, a smart new steely grey pelage is revealed. As a result, individuals which are moulting often have a rather mottled appearance, with contrasting areas of grey and brown hair. Studies of wild common seals have so far been unable to define the exact length of the moult period, but hair is probably lost over a period of up to three or four weeks. This is just the final stage of a much longer series of events which constitute the moult cycle, however, and it has been suggested that the entire period of regression, shedding and regeneration of hair may take between four and six months.

It is likely that there is a high degree of individual variation in both the pattern of hair loss and the length of time over which this loss occurs. In addition, there are marked age- and sex-related differences in the timing of moult. Yearling common seals show the first signs of moult and some can be seen starting to lose hair as early as the first half of June. Older seals start shedding in the middle of July and by early August most seals seen ashore at haul-out sites show some sign of moult. Females moult first and, on average, have shed all their old hair by the middle of August. Large mature males, those showing signs of neck wounds and scars, are the last to lose their old hair, with younger males falling in between the two extremes. The reasons for these variations in timing are not understood fully but it seems likely that the timing of an individual's moult is related in some way to levels of its reproductive hormones.

During the period of hair loss, common seals often appear surprisingly reluctant to enter the water and can be approached more closely on land than at other times of year. Radio-tracking studies have shown that, amongst males at least, common seals show a very marked change in behaviour during this period. A week or two before they show any obvious sign of hair loss, individual males start to haul out every day. In areas where haul-out sites are always available, they remain ashore for long periods throughout the day, entering the water only to feed for a short period during the night. For male common seals then, this is the time of year when they are most tied to land and when they spend least time in the water. The primary function of this increase in time ashore is believed to be to maintain a high skin temperature, which speeds up the growth of the epidermal cells. Similar changes in behaviour are also found amongst other phocids, the most extreme example being the elephant seals *Mirounga leonina* and *M. angustirostris*, which remain ashore throughout the moult, fasting for the whole period. Radio-tracking data on the behaviour of female common seals during the moult period are more limited, but females do not seem to haul out as regularly or for such long periods as the males. Instead, it appears that females have to feed more intensively at this time to replace the fat resources that they have used up during lactation. As a result, the females' moult period may be more protracted, with the early stages occurring when they are spending more time on land with their pups.

Feeding ecology

Common seals are superb divers and take all their food underwater. It is this ability which makes their feeding ecology such an interesting topic for study and yet it also makes such studies difficult to carry out. Except in rather atypical situations, for example around fishing nets, their feeding activity has been observed only rarely in the wild. It is therefore not possible to use direct observations to study common seal feeding ecology. Instead, food remains have to be collected to identify the prey species and techniques such as radio-tracking used to discover when and where seals feed.

DIVING BEHAVIOUR

It is their ability to make prolonged dives, and to spend a high proportion of their time foraging underwater, that has allowed seals to exploit food resources not available to most other mammals. Several adaptations permit them to go for long periods without breathing. Seal blood has a much higher haemoglobin concentration than that of terrestrial mammals and, together with high muscle concentrations of myoglobin, another protein which combines with oxygen, this allows large amounts of oxygen to be stored during a dive. In addition seals have high blood volumes for their body size, with a greatly enlarged venous system to store it, and blood flow can be restricted to vital areas when seals are below the surface. Seals also have a bi-modal heart-rate pattern. When underwater, common seal heart rate is about forty beats per minute, but this rises to around 120 beats per minute as soon as the seal comes to the surface to breath. In an emergency the heart rate can drop much lower, to less than ten beats per minute, and adult common seals have survived forced dives for up to thirty minutes by respiring anaerobically. This classic 'bradycardia', when the heart rate drops to very low levels, is, however, probably quite atypical in the wild. Instead, dives are mostly aerobic and the diving heart rate should perhaps be seen as the normal rate, with the faster surface rate being a mechanism to load up with oxygen as quickly as possible before they go down for the next dive.

As a result of these adaptations, common seals can make repeated aerobic dives, generally between three and eight minutes long, for many hours. Data on dive times can be collected by listening to radio-tagged seals, as the radio signal can be heard only during the period when the seal is at the surface. Longer dives of about ten minutes have also been recorded from radio-tagged common seals, particularly when they were resting in shallow water or 'bottling' — repeatedly surfacing at the same spot and then sinking to the bottom to rest. Dives often appear to be very regular, with a series of similar-length dives and 10 to 20 per cent of the dive time spent at the surface between each dive.

Techniques for recording the depths to which seals dive were developed in the mid 1980s, but only very preliminary results are available. Common seals which were followed around Orkney by the Sea Mammal Research Unit repeatedly dived down to a depth of over 50 metres to the sea-bed, and it seems likely that they could dive down much further in deeper water. The deepest dive recorded for a common seal is much deeper than this but is only circumstantial: a record of an adult seal caught in a fish trap off the coast of California at a depth of over 500 metres. Further studies using depth recorders may be able to confirm whether such deep dives are typical.

DIET

It is possible to identify the prey of common seals by looking for prey remains in either the seals' stomach contents or in their faeces. Remains found in stomachs may sometimes be intact enough to recognise fish species from external characteristics but, in most studies, prey have to be identified from their skeletal remains. In particular, the fish ear bones, or otoliths, and squid 'beaks' have proved very important for assessing the diet of seals, as well as that of other marine predators such as seabirds and large fish. Otoliths from different fish species are quite characteristic and, within each species, the size of otolith is related to overall body size. Therefore, not only can the prey species be identified, but some assessment can be made of the size of the fish that the seal has eaten. Nevertheless, these techniques are not without their problems. The heads of large fish, which include the otoliths, may not always be consumed and some prey species may therefore be missed. Certain fish species have relatively small otoliths and these are more likely to be degraded as they pass through the seal's gut; consequently these are also less likely to be found in the faeces. In addition, defecation probably occurs most commonly in the water and faecal samples collected at terrestrial haul-out sites may not be typical if seals are concentrating their feeding activity further offshore. On the other hand, data resulting from the

21. *A scarred adult male hauled out in the early stages of his moult.*

22. *A radio-tagged adult male. These radio transmitters can be used to study the diving patterns and feeding movements of common seals.*

collection of stomachs are not necessarily any more reliable. In the past many of the seals shot at haul-out sites for diet analysis had empty stomachs, while those taken at sea have generally been shot around fishing nets. Consequently, food remains found in these samples are also unlikely to be typical. In practice, all methods involved in the assessment of diet are likely to involve many biases so it is essential that these biases are evaluated fully before interpreting the results.

Few studies have been carried out on the diet of common seals in British waters. Nevertheless, a wide variety of prey has been identified. Although squid and crustacean remains are sometimes found, most prey species appear to be fish. These include members of the gadoid, clupeoid, pleuronectid and salmonid families such as cod (*Gadus morrhua*), herring (*Clupea harengus*), plaice (*Pleuronectes platessa*) and salmon (*Salmo salar*). However, due to the potential biases in the techniques used to assess diet, as already outlined, it is not possible to evaluate accurately the relative importance of the different prey species. Comparisons with studies on common seal populations elsewhere suggest that common seals are opportunist feeders, taking advantage of prey which are locally abundant. Therefore, the composition of their diet is likely to vary between seasons and between different parts of their range. Furthermore, as a result of the massive fluctuations in the size of many fish populations, the diet of common seals may also vary considerably from one year to the next.

FEEDING ACTIVITY

Because their haul-out sites occur in sheltered inshore waters, it has generally been believed that common seals also feed in those same areas. However, with the development of suitable radio-tracking techniques it has been discovered that, at certain times of year, they spend much of their time foraging outside these areas. In the summer, when common seals are breeding and moulting, they do seem to spend a high proportion of their time close to the haul-out sites. During the winter, in contrast, individuals may leave these inshore areas for periods ranging from several days to a couple of weeks, although they still return inshore to haul out and rest between feeding trips. Although it is possible to be sure that seals have moved away from the waters around haul-out sites, locating radio-tagged seals while they are at sea is more problematic. Consequently it is still unclear exactly where and how far common seals go to feed.

These seasonal changes in activity patterns are of interest when compared with studies of seasonal changes in the body condition and blubber reserves of common seals. Such work suggests that it is during the winter period that common seals are fattest and that this is when the most successful feeding activity occurs. On the other hand, both males and females often appear much thinner during the late summer. It may therefore be that their dependence on land during the breeding season and moult restricts them to feeding in less productive inshore waters during the summer, so that they have to rely on stored body fat over this period. Alternatively, increased winter feeding activity may be a response to a seasonal increase in food availability.

Almost nothing is known of how common seals locate and catch their prey, or of the details of their underwater feeding behaviour. Very large fish are sometimes brought to the surface to be shaken apart and eaten. However, intact herring and saithe (*Pollachius virens*) up to 30 centimetres long have been found in common seal stomachs and most prey up to this size are probably swallowed whole underwater. One point of particular interest is how seals locate their prey. As stated above, seals appear to be able to feed at considerable depths, where ambient light levels are very low. In addition, there is some evidence that common seals tend to feed at night, possibly because changes in the schooling behaviour of their prey make prey capture easier. Common seal vision is good in both air and water and may be good enough to locate prey even at low light intensities, especially if prey are located from below against the brighter surface waters. Alternatively, their whiskers are very sensitive and could be used to detect vibrations from swimming fish.

21

Interactions with man

Historically, seals have played an important part in the economy and folklore of people living around the coast of Britain, although it is often unclear whether accounts relate to common seals or grey seals. Seal bones, mostly from grey seals, have been found in middens from as far back as the neolithic period. Subsistence hunting of both species continued in many areas well into the twentieth century, with seals being killed primarily for their skins and oil, and occasionally for their meat. Seal skins had a number of traditional uses, including shoes, threshing flails and saddle covers. Oil was used in lamps in many areas and was also fed to cattle in more recent times. In the seventeenth century the church considered that seals were fish and people were allowed to eat seal meat during Lent and on other fast days. Eventually the bishops ruled against this, and the consumption of seal meat became confined to the poorer folk who salted it and hung it in their chimneys to be smoked. In many areas, however, people regarded seals with a certain amount of fear and killed them only out of necessity. This often arose from a belief in the selkies — seals which could discard their skins and take up a human form, often only to be drawn back to the sea after stealing the heart of a local lad. Such selkie legends abound around Orkney and Shetland, down the west coast of Britain and Ireland and also in similar coastal populations in North America.

During the twentieth century subsistence hunting for seals in Britain has all but disappeared and interactions between seals and man have fallen into three main areas: commercial hunting for skins, interactions related to the perceived competition between seals and fisheries, and the potential effects on seals of pollution resulting from industrial activity. In addition, common seals can be an important tourist attraction in some areas, either where boat trips take visitors to see their haul-out sites or where captive seals are displayed in zoos and aquaria.

COMMERCIAL HUNTING

Seal skins have been among the exports from areas such as Orkney and Shetland since at least the seventeenth century. In the twentieth century, the trade in common seal skins increased in the late 1950s. This followed a move by salmon netsmen in north-east Scotland to pay hunters to come and shoot pups, as it was believed that common seals were damaging the local fishery. Hunting activity in Shetland and the Wash also increased at this time but, as there were no controls on the number of pups taken, no official records exist of the numbers killed. However, by the late 1960s, the low numbers of common seals seen at haul-out sites in Shetland suggested that this population was being over-exploited and the Conservation of Seals Act (1970) was brought in to restrict hunting. This act provided closed seasons for both common and grey seals in their respective breeding seasons. During these closed seasons pups could be killed only under licence from the Secretary of State for Scotland and the number of pups killed had to be reported. The act also included the provision to issue total protection orders and, in 1973, common seal hunting was banned completely in Shetland; this was followed by a ban on hunting in the Wash in 1974. The legislation has changed only slightly since then, with the Conservation of Seals Act being incorporated into the Wildlife and Countryside Act (1981), and no further licences have been issued allowing anyone to take common seal pups for their skins. Furthermore, owing to changing public opinion, the value of seal skins has dropped markedly and future hunting is unlikely to be worthwhile on economic grounds.

INTERACTIONS BETWEEN SEALS AND FISHERIES

During the 1970s and 1980s there has been much controversy over the potential effects of seal populations on commercial fisheries. While the debate has centred around the management of the British grey seal population, common seals have also been accused of causing damage to

22

fisheries and bounties have been paid for killing them in certain areas in an attempt to reduce damage levels.

Two main types of interaction occur between seals and fisheries: operational and biological. Operational or interference interactions are those where seals damage fishing gear or take fish directly from nets. The effect of these interactions can be considerable for individual fishermen, because of the cost of repairing equipment and the reduced income from lost or damaged fish. In the past most damage of this kind occurred around salmon-netting stations on the east coast of Britain and other static fishing gear such as long-lines. In the 1980s, with the increase in salmon farms in Scottish waters, seals have also been reported to cause damage to farmed salmon by attacking fish through the cages. In many instances it is not known whether grey or common seals are the main culprits, or whether it is just particular 'rogue' individuals who specialise in feeding in such situations. It is therefore unclear whether culling the population of either species would be cost-effective or produce any significant benefits to the fishermen. Instead, most research in this area is concentrating on protecting nets and farms more effectively, for example by improving the design of anti-predator nets or by using non-lethal acoustic scaring devices.

The nature and extent of biological interactions between seals and fisheries are much more difficult to evaluate. These interactions involve ecological competition between man and seals, where seals may be eating fish which would otherwise be available for the commercial fishery to catch. Conversely, it is also possible that over-exploitation of certain stocks by commercial fisheries could lead to food shortages for seals and other marine wildlife. The extent of these interactions depends not only on what species of fish the seals take, but also on the age of those fish, how much they consume each day and whether they are feeding in areas that are fished by commercial boats. Seals may even cause some benefits to fisheries, for example if they were feeding primarily on large predatory species which in turn took fish which were especially important in the commercial catch. These interactions are therefore extremely complex and, unfortunately, rather poorly understood. As discussed in the previous chapter, there are not even adequate data on the proportion of different prey species in the diet of common seals. Neither is there reliable information on the daily energy requirements of common seals. Consequently, current attempts to assess the extent of biological interactions between common seals and British fisheries are almost entirely speculative. Even when suitable data become available to assess these interactions, it is likely that any major decisions regarding the management of British seal populations will be made largely on political grounds.

POLLUTANTS AND SEALS

Like many other top predators, common seals have been found to contain high levels of certain pollutants. In particular, fat-soluble organochlorine compounds such as DDT and the industrial polychlorinated biphenyls (PCBs) may occur at high levels in common seal blubber. Compared with terrestrial top predators, such as the predatory birds, the effects of these high organochlorine levels on the health of marine mammals are poorly understood. Nevertheless, there is now experimental evidence from Holland that female common seals fed with fish with high (though 'naturally' occurring) PCB levels have a lowered reproductive capacity. The exact mechanism causing these reproductive failures is not known, but this work does support the suggestion that high levels of pollution in the eastern North Sea may have contributed to the decline of the Dutch common seal population which was observed during the 1950s and 1960s. High levels of organochlorines may also suppress an animal's immune system, possibly making seals with high PCB levels more vulnerable to disease.

A number of heavy metal compounds have also been found in common seals. Tissue levels of mercury have been most studied and, in some cases, these have been much higher than one would expect a mammal to be able to tolerate. Seals appear to be able to survive such high levels by detoxifying the mercury that they consume; mercury found in fish is generally in its most toxic form, methyl mercury, whereas most mercury in seals is stored in their livers as inorganic mercury. Some of the highest levels of mercury in both marine mammals and seabirds have been found in animals from relatively clean waters, such as the Antarctic. It is therefore likely that the mercury found in many of these species is from naturally occurring sources, and that seals have evolved a mechanism to detoxify these harmful compounds as a result of living in areas of high background mercury. Several studies have shown that mercury and selenium occur in the ratio of 1:1 in seal livers, suggesting that selenium may be involved in this detoxification process.

There are also a few records of seals becoming contaminated with oil, and one report from France of a young common seal which apparently died as a result of ingesting crude oil. Various other kinds of discarded waste, such as pieces of old fishing net, may also cause some deaths. Common seals are sometimes seen with pieces of net caught around their necks; if this happens when they are still growing they could eventually die. In some areas of the Pacific large numbers of marine mammals and seabirds are known to die after becoming caught in discarded nets. Fortunately, this particular problem does not appear to be very great in the Atlantic.

Further reading

Anderson, Sheila. *The Grey Seal*. Shire Natural History 26, Shire Publications, 1988. Companion volume to this publication and very useful for comparison between the two British species.

Hewer, H. R. *British Seals*. Collins New Naturalist, 1974. Now out of print and rather dated. Concentrates on the biology of the grey seal more than the common seal.

King, J. E. *Seals of the World*. British Museum (Natural History) and Oxford University Press, 1983. A good general guide to seal biology with individual accounts for each species.

Thomson, D. *The People of the Sea*. Barrie and Rockcliffe, 1965. Stories based on the selkie legends. Now available in paperback from Paladin.

ACKNOWLEDGEMENTS
Illustrations are acknowledged as follows: Sarah Jackson, 1, 5, 9; J. Lawson, 15; Tessa Lovatt-Smith, 10, 17, 18; A. R. Martin, 13; Beth Perry, 16; P. Reynolds, 14; R. Tidman, 8. All other illustrations are by the author.